OCT 2015

EXPLORING
CAREERS

Careers in the Military

Barbara Sheen

ReferencePoint
Press®

San Diego, CA

© 2015 ReferencePoint Press, Inc.
Printed in the United States

For more information, contact:
ReferencePoint Press, Inc.
PO Box 27779
San Diego, CA 92198
www.ReferencePointPress.com

Picture Credits:
Maury Aaseng: 6
© Ed Darack/Science Faction/Corbis: 18
© Faleh Kheiber/Reuters/Corbis: 28
© Stocktrek Images/Corbis: 66

LIBRARY OF CONGRESS CATALOGING-IN-PUBLICATION DATA

Sheen, Barbara.
  Careers in the Military / by Barbara Sheen.
    pages cm -- (Exploring careers series)
  Includes bibliographical references and index.
  ISBN-13: 978-1-60152-688-5 (hardback)
  ISBN-10: 1-60152-688-1 (hardback)
  1. United States--Armed Forces--Vocational guidance. I. Title.
  UB147.S54 2015
  355.0023'73--dc23
                                                      2014002880

Contents

Many Opportunities

The US military is always hiring. Approximately one thousand new recruits enlist in the military each day, filling new positions and positions vacated by service members who are returning to civilian life. In all, more than 1.5 million men and women are currently part of the US military, making it the nation's largest employer.

The military has a place for all types of individuals. Almost every civilian career has a military counterpart; plus, a wide range of combat careers are specific to the military. In all, the military offers more than two thousand different military occupational specialties (MOS), which are divided into broad categories. These categories include accounting and finance; arts, communication, and media design; aviation; business administration; combat operations; communications equipment technology; construction; and counseling. Education and training; engineering; environmental health and safety; health care; human resources; information technology, and computer science are also included. So are intelligence; international relations and linguistics; law enforcement; legal professions; mechanic; medical technology; maritime operations; personal and food services; and transportation, supply, and logistics.

To determine where a prospective service member's skills lie, before enlisting in the military individuals are required to take the Armed Services Vocational Aptitude Battery (ASVAB) exam. The results are used to match new recruits to the career category that best suits them. Once this is determined, there are a myriad of occupations in each field to choose from. For instance, musicians, heating and cooling mechanics, translators, electricians, store managers, teachers, and graphic designers are all part of the military.

Training

To ensure service members succeed in their chosen profession, they are given extensive training. Moreover, throughout their military career service members are given opportunities to continue training in their original field or in other fields. Ongoing training allows service members to change career fields if they so desire. In all, the military offers about ten thousand specialized training courses. In addition, the military pays up to $3,500 per year in college tuition for service members who take college classes while serving in the military.

Military training is far reaching. It can be used to gain civilian licenses in careers such as software engineer or electrician, among others. And it can translate into related civilian careers. As Army helicopter mechanic Corey Lutzow explains on Careers in the Military, a website sponsored by the US government: "The training I have received in the military is priceless. Apart from my technical training that allows me to diagnose and repair aircraft, I have learned many other valuable skills; for example, how to work effectively as a team in order to successfully accomplish a mission; how to be an effective leader; and how to be confident and never second guess myself."

Five Branches

Besides choosing a career path, enlistees must decide on which branch of the military they want to join. There are five branches of the US military: the Army, the Navy, the Air Force, the Marine Corps, and the Coast Guard. All five branches are responsible for protecting the security of the United States. Each offers the same pay scale, and many career specialties are duplicated among the branches.

Which branch a person joins is a personal choice. The Army is the oldest and largest branch of the military. Traditionally, it is known as the branch that fights on land, although today's Army is also involved in aviation. The Navy helps to protect the nation's freedom of the seas. Naval personnel live and work on ships and submarines for long periods of time. They also serve in aviation positions and on bases on land. The Air Force defends US airways. Air Force members fly and maintain many different types of aircraft and aviation equipment. Individuals interested in aviation, technology, and mechanical professions are often drawn to the Air Force. The Marine Corps operates on sea, land, and air. Marines are usually the advance troops in military operations. They also provide security at naval bases and

Military Job Outlook

Active Duty Enlisted Personnel by Broad Occupational Group, June 2013

Enlisted Occupational group	Army	Air Force	Coast Guard	Marine Corps	Navy	Total enlisted personnel in each occupational group
Administrative occupations	6,042	14,946	1,546	12,268	19,147	53,949
Combat Specialty occupations	122,254	581	636	43,707	8,219	175,397
Construction occupations	18,144	5,647	—	6,102	4,410	34,303
Electronic and Electrical Equipment Repair occupations	35,203	32,359	4,633	17,561	46,387	136,143
Engineering, Science, and Technical occupations	44,873	49,557	1,272	28,472	38,923	163,097
Health Care occupations	32,199	16,638	730	—	26,253	75,820
Human Resource Development occupations	16,608	8,292	1	2,284	3,956	31,141
Machine Operator and Production occupations	4,615	6,609	1,886	2,711	8,353	24,174
Media and Public Affairs occupations	7,643	6,870	141	2,561	1,882	19,097
Protective Service occupations	25,167	35,695	2,828	6,359	11,378	81,427
Support Service occupations	11,086	5,744	1,239	2,441	7,901	28,411
Transportation and Material Handling occupations	53,833	31,935	10,284	24,396	37,246	157,694
Vehicle and Machinery Mechanic occupations	49,237	44,634	5,641	21,806	46,551	167,869
Non-occupation or unspecified coded personnel	2,984	4,722	1,531	2,100	2,966	14,303
Total enlisted personnel for each military branch	429,888	264,229	32,368	172,768	263,572	1,162,825

Active Duty Enlisted Personnel by Broad Occupational Group (Excluding Coast Guard), June 2013

Officer Occupational group	Army	Air Force	Coast Guard	Marine Corps	Navy	Total officer personnel in each occupational group
Combat Specialty occupations	23,312	3,870	—	4,649	5,845	37,676
Engineering, Science, and Technical occupations	25,343	16,238	—	4,375	9,720	55,676
Executive, Administration, and Managerial occupations	14,716	7,275	—	3,025	6,942	31,958
Health Care occupations	12,192	9,286	—		6,382	27,860
Human Resource Development occupations	3,172	1,940	—	271	3,189	8,572
Media and Public Affairs occupations	388	327	—	206	256	1,177
Protective Service occupations	3,145	1,146	—	414	991	5,696
Support Service occupations	1,782	716	—	41	939	3,478
Transportation occupations	13,055	19,782	—	6,484	11,025	50,346
Non-occupation or unspecified coded personnel	2,686	4,523	—	2,575	8,967	18,751
Total officer personnel for each military branch	99,791	65,103	8,659	22,040	54,256	249,849

Source: Bureau of Labor Statistics, US Department of Labor, Occupational Outlook Handbook, 2014–15 Edition,

US embassies and consulates around the world. The Coast Guard is the smallest branch of the military. Coast Guard personnel serve on ships, on aircraft, and in ports. They protect US coasts, coastal waters, and inland waterways.

Enlisted Personnel or Officers

In order to enlist in the military, individuals must have a high school diploma, be between the ages of seventeen and thirty-five (twenty-five for the Air Force), and pass a physical exam. Candidates may be screened out because they do not meet height or weight requirements or, depending on the branch of the military, because they possess a criminal record.

Individuals accepted into the military enter the service as either enlisted personnel or officers (also known as commissioned officers). Enlisted personnel carry out the daily operations of the military. Officers lead and manage enlisted personnel. Generally, the difference between the requirements for enlisted personnel and officers is that officers have a bachelor's degree or higher. However, warrant officers, highly specialized officers with expertise in certain technical fields, are not required to have a college degree.

There are nine enlisted grades, five warrant officer ranks, and ten officer ranks. A service member's pay is dependent on his or her grade or rank, and promotions depend on an individual's years of service, ability, and length of time since their last promotion. Upon earning a bachelor's degree, enlisted personnel can be promoted to commissioned officers.

A Binding Contract

Enlisting in the military is a binding commitment. The length of the commitment depends on the branch of the military and the type of duty selected. There are two types of duty: active duty, in which individuals serve as full-time service members, and reserve duty. All five branches of the military have reserve forces. The Army and Air Force also have National Guard branches. National Guard members are reservists who serve as homeland defenders under the authority of each state's governor and the Department of Defense. Reservists serve part-time, training one weekend per month and two full weeks per year while pursuing a civilian career. All reservists, including members of the National Guard, may be called up for active duty if the need arises. Between 2001 and 2004, for example, 247,181 reservists were called to active-duty service in Iraq and Afghanistan. Service members can sign up to serve the first part of their contract on active duty and the remainder on reserve duty. Or they may serve solely on active duty or in the reserves.

Whether on active duty or in the reserves, once individuals enlist in the military they cannot quit until their term of duty is up. Life in the military is not for everyone. It is regimented, and service members are expected to follow rules and obey orders. But for the many men and women dedicated to serving their country, the challenges and rewards of a military career far outweigh any disadvantages. Many feel like Lutzow, who says: "I think I'll serve 20 years in the military, maybe more if they'll let me. I really love what I do and could not think of anything better."

Automotive and Heavy Equipment Mechanic

What Does an Automotive and Heavy Equipment Mechanic Do?

Automotive and heavy equipment mechanics maintain and repair combat vehicles and construction equipment such as jeeps, aircraft-towing vehicles, tanks, and bulldozers. They also work on trucks, backhoes, tractors, and power shovels, among other high- and low-tech equipment. As an article on the US Air Force's website explains: "Anybody can work on cars, but few have the skills and attention to detail needed to work on multimillion-dollar military vehicles. As a Vehicle and Vehicular Equipment Maintenance specialist [another name for an automotive and heavy equipment mechanic], you'll be trained to work on everything from snow blowers and dump trucks to forklifts and aircraft towing vehicles. Whether it's a gas or diesel engine, a transmission, drive train or even an air conditioning system, your expertise will be vital to not only repairing problems, but also to prevent them as well."

Using a variety of state-of-the-art test equipment as well as their own eyes and ears, these professionals systematically analyze vehicular problems. Then they make repairs. No part of a vehicle is too complex for their skills and training. They work on transmissions, engines, tires, and electrical systems. Repairing drive trains, including brakes and suspension systems; hydraulic, heating, and air-conditioning systems; and emission controls is also part of their job. In a typical day these mechanics may inspect and perform routine maintenance and repairs on a jeep, tune up a truck, or repair a diesel or gasoline engine. They may recover a combat vehicle that has broken down in the field or perform emergency repairs to the vehicle in the field. Hoisting and jacking up heavy equipment is also part of their job. So is performing a complete engine overhaul, and test-driving vehicles. Doing body work to damaged vehicles is another of their responsibilities. Keeping maintenance records on the vehicles they service, monitoring repair orders and the use of parts, and conducting on-the-job training for new mechanics may also be a part of an average day.

Automotive and heavy equipment mechanics work in all five branches of the military. They are also known as engineer equipment mechanics in the Marine Corps, construction mechanics in the Navy, vehicle and vehicular equipment maintenance personnel in the Air Force, and machinery technicians in the Coast Guard. These service men and women may work on every type of wheel or track vehicles; or those serving in the Army, Air Force, and Marines may specialize. However, there are no subspecialties for this career in the Navy and Coast Guard. Army specialty fields include wheeled vehicle mechanic, track vehicle repairer, M-1 Abrams tank maintainer, and land combat electronic missile system repairer. Air Force specialties include special vehicle maintenance. Marine specialties include automotive organizational mechanic and logistic systems mechanic.

Army wheeled vehicle mechanics and Marine automotive organizational mechanics repair and maintain wheeled vehicles, while track vehicle repairers work on tanks and other track vehicles. M-1 Abrams tank maintainers limit their work to a specific tank, the highly complex Abrams tank. Land combat electronic missile system repairers maintain and repair vehicles with anti-tank missile systems. Air Force special vehicle maintenance involves the maintenance and repair of all ground vehicles used in support of aircraft, while Marine logistics vehicle systems mechanics inspect, diagnose, and maintain special eight-wheel all-terrain vehicles.

How Do You Become an Automotive and Heavy Equipment Mechanic?

Education

Automotive and heavy equipment mechanics are enlisted service members. As such, they are required to have a high school diploma. To prepare for this career, high school students should take classes in auto mechanics and technology, computer technology, mathematics, physical education, and English. The last is important because these professionals must be able to read and understand service manuals without any problems.

Once service members complete basic training, the military provides all the instruction they need to become automotive and heavy equipment mechanics. Training can last from eight to twenty-nine weeks depending on the specialty. In many cases trainees can earn college credit for their training. For instance, Air Force personnel who successfully complete seventy-nine days of training for this career earn eleven hours of college credit. Instruction includes classroom and hands-on training in the principles of gasoline, diesel, and turbine engines, as well as in engine tune-ups and repairs. Students also learn about electrical starting and charging systems, hydraulics, body repair and body panel replacement, soldering, and heating and cooling systems. Other training specific to armored vehicles includes instruction in the mechanical principles of tanks, drive trains of track vehicles, and using diagnostic and testing equipment in tank repair. Interpreting and using wiring diagrams and operating, testing, and maintaining weapon systems in tanks is also covered. Once service members have completed their course of study, they receive on-the-job training under the supervision of experienced mechanics.

Throughout their career, these service members are given the opportunity to hone their skills with ongoing advanced training. Among other options, they can opt for instruction in new advances in equipment and technology, working with specialized vehicles, or in leadership training. The latter often includes classes in designing vehicle repair shop workstations, managing a vehicle repair facility, supervising facility personnel, and making and assigning work schedules.

Certification and Licensing

This profession does not require any certification or licenses. However, the training these specialists receive can help them get credentials or certification from the National Institute for Automotive Service Excellence, an organization that licenses civilian mechanics. Obtaining these credentials helps service members earn promotion points that can accelerate their eligibility for promotion. Having these credentials also helps veterans gain employment upon leaving the military. Certificates include Automotive/Light Truck: Automatic Transmission/Transaxle, Automotive/Light Truck: Brakes, Automotive/Light Truck: Electrical/Electronic Systems, and Automotive/Light Truck: Engine Performance. Applicants must pass a test to gain each certification. Reimbursement for exam fees is provided by the federal government.

Volunteer Work and Internships

Young people interested in a career as a mechanic in the military can learn about what military life is like by participating in Junior Reserve Officer Training Corps (Jr. ROTC) in high school. Jr. ROTC members receive course credit for participating and take part in activities such as fitness training, drill teams, and visits to military bases. Participation can help military recruits get through basic training more easily.

Getting a part-time or summer job in an automotive repair shop is another way aspiring automobile and heavy equipment specialists can learn more about the job; so is job shadowing an automobile mechanic for at least one day. Working on family vehicles is also a good way to become more familiar with auto mechanics.

Skills and Personality

Individuals who have a mechanical aptitude and enjoy working with their hands are often drawn to a career as an automotive and heavy equipment mechanic. The work is physically demanding. Therefore, these servicemen and servicewomen should be physically fit. Military mechanics must be able to lift heavy equipment and tools without any problems. They have to stand and bend a lot and keep their arms and hands steady while working. They also should have good eye-hand co-ordination and manual dexterity in order to effectively work with large and small tools and put together small parts with their fingers. More-over, they should enjoy using machines, tools, and mechanical equip-ment. Good eyesight and color vision are also needed to read diagrams and work with color-coded wires. And these professionals should be comfortable working in cramped areas or underneath vehicles.

Mentally, these service members should be good problem solv-ers. An important part of their work is troubleshooting. These profes-sionals should be able to isolate mechanical problems, notice when the problem occurs, figure out what is causing the problem, and de-termine the best way to fix it. This job also requires careful attention to detail. Small errors can cause mechanical malfunctions that can put combat troops in harm's way. In addition, like all service mem-bers, these specialists must be able to obey orders and listen to and understand instructions.

On the Job

Employers

All five branches of the military employ automotive and heavy equip-ment mechanics. These men and women may serve on activity duty or in the reserves.

Working Conditions

Military vehicle mechanics usually work indoors in large repair shops, motor pools, and maintenance units. Garages are located on US mili-tary bases throughout the world. Overseas sites include bases in Af-ghanistan, Iraq, Italy, Germany, Spain, England, Japan, South Korea, and Greenland, among other sites. Large numbers of mechanics typically work close together, and these workplaces are quite noisy.

In addition to working in repair shops, these men and women often make emergency repairs to vehicles in the field. This includes working in combat zones with all the risks that entails.

Earnings

Military pay is standardized. It is based on a service member's rank or grade and time in the service. According to the Department of Defense (DOD), as of 2013 the base salary for active-duty enlisted service members ranges from $16,824 to $89,220. Under certain circumstances, service members may qualify for additional pay. For instance, automotive and heavy equipment mechanics working in a combat zone receive an additional $375 per month for hazardous duty. Moreover, all service members receive multiple opportunities to travel as well as benefits that can add up to a significant amount. Benefits include thirty days of paid vacation per year, free medical and dental care, education benefits, and retirement benefits. The military also provides all active-duty members who live on base with housing and food. Service members living off base receive a food and housing allowance. The amount is based on the service member's rank, family size, and location.

Each branch of the military also offers enlistment bonuses, which vary depending on the military branch, whether the recruit chooses active duty or the reserves, the terms of enlistment, the military career field, and the enlistee's education and qualifications. Bonuses range from about $2,000 to $40,000.

Opportunities for Advancement

Typically, service members receive a raise in pay each time they go up in grade or rank, about every two years. However, servicemen and servicewomen can advance more rapidly based on their job performance, military training, promotion points, ongoing education, and civilian certifications, among other things. An example of a typical career path in this military occupational specialty is that of a Marine sergeant who started his career repairing jeeps and trucks in Camp LeJeune, North Carolina. Because of his good work and ongoing training, he was promoted to shop chief, a position in which he supervised other mechanics. After two years in this position he received another promotion and was reassigned to Okinawa, Japan, where he served as a maintenance chief. In this position he was responsible for maintaining shop safety and for scheduling all vehicles on the base for maintenance. One year later he was reassigned to the United States as an inspector. In this job he traveled throughout the United States inspecting wheeled vehicles at Marine reserve units. After being promoted to gunnery sergeant, the seventh highest enlisted rank in the Marine Corps, he was reassigned to the motor transport department at Marine headquarters in Arlington, Virginia, where he is employed today.

Upon leaving the military, military mechanics often find employment in automobile paint and body shops, automobile dealerships, construction or farm equipment companies, or state highway departments. Some veterans open their own automotive repair shops.

What Is the Future Outlook for Automotive and Heavy Equipment Mechanics?

The military employs about forty-five thousand automotive and heavy equipment mechanics. New mechanics are needed each year to replace personnel returning to civilian life. In addition, the ongoing threat of global terrorism has increased the military's need to maintain and upgrade tanks and other combat vehicles, which increases the need for qualified personnel to care for this equipment.

Find Out More

America's Navy: "Mechanical and Industrial Technology Jobs"
website: www.navy.com

The official website of the Navy offers information about the Navy. The section on mechanical and industrial technology jobs provides information about different mechanical professions in the Navy.

Careers in the Military: "Automotive and Heavy Equipment Mechanic"
website: www.careersinthemilitary.com

This Defense Department website provides information on every branch of the military and military careers. The "Automotive and Heavy Equipment Mechanic" page gives information on the profession and provides a link to other related specialties.

Go Coast Guard: "Machinery Technician (MK)"
website: www.gocoastguard.com

The official Coast Guard website provides information about the Coast Guard and information about a career as a machinery technician (or MK for short), the term used in the Coast Guard for an automotive and heavy equipment mechanic.

US Air Force: "Vehicle and Vehicular Equipment Maintenance"
website: www.airforce.com

This is the official website of the US Air Force. It offers information about the Air Force and different Air Force careers. The page on a career in vehicle and vehicular equipment maintenance provides information on what the job entails.

US Marine Corps: "Roles in the Corps: Motor Transport"
website: www.marines.com

This article on the official website of the Marine Corps provides information about transportation specialty careers in the Marines, including automotive maintenance and a video interview with a Marine motor vehicle operator, a specialty that includes operating and repairing vehicles.

Communications Equipment Operator

The ability to keep communications flowing is critical to national security. In a combat situation it allows commanding officers in military headquarters to get information to troops on the battlefield. Communications equipment operators are vital to this effort. Operating a variety of sophisticated communications equipment, including satellites, radios, microwave communication systems, computer systems, telephones, and complex security devices, they receive, transmit, and log vital communications. They also decode and encode classified messages and handle emergency calls, which occur frequently in combat zones. These specialists also install, repair, and perform preventive maintenance on communication equipment and networks.

In a typical day communication specialists monitor, transmit, and keep a log of hundreds

At a Glance:
Communications Equipment Operator

Minimum Educational Requirements
High school diploma

Personal Qualities
Detail oriented; interest in technology

Certification and Licensing
Secret security clearance

Working Conditions
Indoors or outdoors in all branches of the military

Salary Range
Basic pay from about $16,824 to $89,220

Number of Jobs
As of 2013 about 40,000

Future Job Outlook
Good

A US Marine communications equipment operator listens to radio transmissions during a training exercise. These military personnel must be well versed in using various specialized radios and in different communications techniques.

of messages sent between troops stationed all over the world. The messages, which often contain information that can change the outcome of a military mission, must be transmitted quickly and accurately. This is not a simple task. Sometimes the messages are classified. In this case, these specialists must put the messages into code before transmitting them. Other complications arise when messages get lost in transmission. As Naval communications equipment officer Staci Guercio explains in an article on the Careers in the Military website: "Many times messages get 'stuck' or lost in transmission and I am responsible for troubleshooting the problem to ensure the message gets properly transmitted in a highly time sensitive matter. Often times, the messages are classified and need special handling. When these messages come through, it is my role to take immediate action and route the message to the proper recipient securely and keep an accurate log of such messages."

These service members operate land and mobile radios, switchboards, digital multichannel equipment, satellite systems, computers, and computer networks. They also install, repair, and perform preventive maintenance on the equipment. Monitoring air traffic control and missile tracking and radar systems may also be part of their daily job. So too is supervising large communication centers.

Communications equipment operators are also known as telecommunications specialists or operations specialists in the Coast Guard. Depending on their training, communications personnel may be qualified to work with a wide range of communication equipment, or they may specialize in one type of equipment. For instance, Army satellite communications systems operators-maintainers, Navy information systems technicians, and Marine satellite communication terminal operators operate and maintain satellite communication systems. Army radio operators-maintainers, Marine field radio operators, and Air Force radio communication systems apprentices work solely with radio communications equipment.

How Do You Become a Communications Equipment Operator?

Education

Communications equipment operators are enlisted personnel. As such, they are required to have a high school diploma. To prepare for the profession, high school students should take classes in computer technology, English, speech, and physical education. Once service members complete basic training, the military provides specific training for the profession. Training takes from nine to twenty-two weeks and includes classroom lectures as well as hands-on practice with communications equipment. Instruction includes courses on the installation, use, maintenance, and repair of various types of equipment. This includes training in mechanical and electronic principles, wiring techniques, and the operation of diagnostic equipment. Communication security policies and procedures, military codes, and encoding and decoding messages are also covered.

Certification and Licensing

No certification or licensing is required for this profession. However, because these service members handle classified messages, they must have secret security clearance. Gaining secret security clearance indicates that an individual is loyal to the United States and able to be trusted with sensitive information that could cause damage to the nation if it is leaked. To get secret security clearance, applicants must be US citizens. They must not have a police record. And they must pass an intensive background check.

Although the military does not require these professionals to hold a special license or certification, the specialized training they receive in the military can help them obtain civilian certifications. Obtaining such credentials helps service members earn promotion points that can accelerate their eligibility for promotion. These credentials help veterans gain employment upon leaving the military. Credentials include certification as an associate electronics technician from the Electronics Technician Association International and certification as an associate computing professional from the Institute for Certification for Computing Professionals. Applicants must pass a test to gain each certification, and they must demonstrate ability in their field. Reimbursement for exam fees is provided by the government.

Volunteer Work and Internships

Young people interested in a career as a communications equipment operator can learn about military life by participating in Junior Reserve Officer Training Corps (Jr. ROTC) in high school. Participation helps keep individuals physically fit, which can help recruits get through basic training more easily. In addition to fitness training, Jr. ROTC members receive course credit for participating and take part in activities such as drill teams and visits to military bases.

Job shadowing a civilian communications equipment operator is another way individuals can learn more about this career field. These individuals may work for telecommunication companies.

Skills and Personality

Military communications equipment operators must have good eyesight and hearing, normal color vision, good eye-hand coordination, and good communication skills. They should enjoy working with electrical and mechanical systems as well as computers, satellite systems, and other high-tech equipment. Being logical and a good problem solver are also essential. These two traits are helpful in troubleshooting problems with equipment or lost messages, as well as in working with codes.

Staying calm under pressure is also important. Monitoring communication is a nonstop chore. Communication channels must be kept open day and night. Messages must be transmitted, received, and logged without error or delays. And, since the messages keep coming, once a message is handled, they must move on rapidly to the next message. There is little respite. Many lives depend on what these professionals do. Therefore, in order to do their job effectively these specialists must be able to stay calm no matter how intense the situation.

In addition, these service members often work as part of a team. Consequently, being able to work well with others and take and follow orders from superior officers are also important traits for these professionals.

On the Job

Employers

All five branches of the military employ communications equipment operators. These men and women may serve as active military or in the reserves.

Working Conditions

These service members work indoors and outdoors. They may work aboard ships or aircraft, in message centers on military bases, or in mobile field units. Mobile field units include four-wheel drive vehicles, armored vehicles, or other military vehicles that may be located in combat zones or hostile territory. Depending on the specialty and the work environment, these professionals may be required to sit for long periods of time. They often work in close physical proximity to other communication equipment operators.

Since messages are received and transmitted whenever they come in and delaying transmission can result in grave consequences, military message centers are manned twenty-four hours a day, seven days a week. Usually service members work in rotating shifts. A typical shift involves working three twelve-hour days with two days off, followed by two twelve-hour workdays with three days off. Many people like working these shifts. They say it gives them time to take college classes, spend time with their families, or just have fun. Shifts are usually divided into day or night shifts and may include holidays and weekends.

Earnings

Military pay is standardized. It is based on a service member's rank or grade and time in the service. According to the Department of Defense (DOD), as of 2013 the base salary for active-duty enlisted service members ranged from $16,824 to $89,220. In addition, service members may qualify for extra pay or bonuses. For instance, communications equipment operators stationed in a combat zone receive an extra $375 per month for hazardous duty. Moreover, all service members receive multiple opportunities to travel as well as paid benefits that can add up to a significant amount. Benefits include thirty days of paid vacation per year, free medical and dental care, education benefits, and retirement benefits. The military also provides all active-duty members who live on base with housing and food. Service members who live off base receive a food and housing allowance. The amount is based on the service member's rank, family size, and location.

Each branch of the military also offers enlistment bonuses, which vary depending on the military branch, whether the recruit chooses active duty or the reserves, the terms of enlistment, the military career, and the enlistee's education and qualifications. Bonuses range from about $2,000 to $40,000. Reenlistment bonuses are also offered to troops in high-demand military careers. Currently, microwave systems operators/maintainers and satellite communication systems operators/maintainers are included in this group. Individuals with these careers who reenlist for three or more years qualify for a bonus ranging from $3,000 to $15,000.

Opportunities for Advancement

The military provides service members many opportunities for advancement. Typically, service members receive a raise in pay each time they go up in grade or rank. On average, this occurs about every two years. However, troops can advance more rapidly depending on an individual's years in the military, job performance, military training, ongoing education, and civilian certifications, among other things. By taking college classes at the military's expense, opting for advanced military training in communications operation and maintenance or in other military fields, and gaining civilian certification such as those offered by the Electronics Technician Association International or the Institute for Certification for Computing Professionals, communications equipment operators can advance quickly. Moreover, if enlisted personnel obtain a bachelor's degree while serving in the military, they can be promoted to commissioned officer. This entitles them to a significant pay raise.

Upon leaving the military, communication specialists can qualify for careers with cable television companies, telephone companies, telecommunication companies, and other businesses, as well as airports and police stations. To connect the business community with the military and help veterans gain civilian employment, the Army, in conjunction with a number of private corporations, sponsors the Partnership for Youth Success (PaYS) program. Service members who opt to participate in the PaYS program are trained by the Army for careers in partner businesses. Upon leaving the military, the participating companies give these trained service members preference in hiring. For communications equipment operators, these corporations include Comcast Cable, Cisco Systems, T-Mobile, Cox Communications, and L-3 Communications. In addition, having held secret security clearance helps veterans gain employment in the private sector. Secret security clearance is difficult to obtain. Therefore, individuals who have held secret security clearance are sought after for a variety of positions in private industry.

What Is the Future Outlook for Communications Equipment Operators?

The military employs about forty thousand communications equipment operators. As personnel leave the military or switch between military careers, the service needs to fill the positions they vacate. Therefore, new recruits are constantly needed. In addition, the ongoing threat of global terrorism has increased the military's need to have trained, able personnel in almost all military occupational specialties including communications.

Find Out More

Careers in the Military: "Communications Equipment Operators"
website: www.careersinthemilitary.com

This DOD website provides information on every branch of the military and military career. The "Communications Equipment Operators" page gives information on the profession and provides a link to an interview with a communications equipment operator.

Go Army: "Computers and Technology Careers"
website: www.goarmy.com

The official website of the US Army offers information about every Army career. The "Computers and Technology" careers page has links to articles on a variety of communication operator specialties including radio operator and satellite communications systems operator.

Go Coast Guard: "Operations Specialist (OS)"
website: www.gocoastguard.com

The official website of the US Coast Guard provides a wealth of information about a career in the Coast Guard. The "Operations Specialist" page gives information on this career as well as a link to a video.

**Today's Military: "Communications Equipment
Technologists and Technicians"**
website: www.todaysmilitary.com

This website is produced by the US Department of Defense. It has in-depth information about every branch of the military and military career fields. The web page on "Communications Equipment Technologists and Technicians" provides information about the profession.

US Marine Corps: "Roles in the Corps: Communications"
website: www.marines.com

This article on the official website of the Marine Corps provides information about communication careers in the Marines, including a video interview with a Marine radio operator.

Food Service Specialist

American servicemen and servicewomen eat more than 1 million meals each day. Food service specialists prepare and serve these meals. They also order and inspect food; keep ovens, stoves, and kitchen utensils clean; plan menus, prepare budgets, and cut large slabs of meat to standard cuts. They may provide classroom instruction for aspiring food service specialists or provide on-the-job training for inexperienced food service personnel. Depending on their assignment, they may cook three meals a day for thousands of service members or prepare special dinners for small groups of dignitaries. The food they prepare not only helps keep service members healthy, it lifts their morale and helps them to do their jobs. As food specialist Staff Seargent Guy Winks explains on the Go Army website: "My job is to feed soldiers anyplace, anytime, under any circumstances. If you've been out in the mud and rain and you've been training hard, there's nothing better than a great plate of food."

At a Glance:
Food Service Specialist

Minimum Educational Requirements
High school diploma

Personal Qualities
Enjoy cooking; interest in food and nutrition

Certification and Licensing
None

Working Conditions
Indoors, all five branches of the military

Salary Range
Basic pay from $16,824 to $89,220

Number of Jobs
As of 2013 about 28,000

Future Job Outlook
Good

In a typical day food service specialists may prepare breakfast for a small flight crew heading off on a vital mission or lunch for five thousand crew members on an aircraft carrier. Like butchers, they use cleavers, band saws, and large knives to prepare standard cuts of meat such as steaks, roasts, or chops. They bake breads, rolls, pies, cakes, and other pastries. They fry batches of chicken, grill burgers, and prepare multiple trays of lasagna. They make sauces, stews, and salads. The last may involve cutting pineapples into perfect little rings or carving radishes into rosettes.

They also prepare multicourse holiday meals for thousands of troops and elegant dinners for high-ranking guests and dignitaries. In fact, the White House Mess is run by Navy food specialists. Navy food specialists also run the dining room in the Pentagon.

How Do You Become a Food Service Specialist?

Education

Food service specialists are enlisted personnel. As such, they are required to be high school graduates. To prepare for a career as a food service specialist, high school students should take classes in family and consumer science, health, physical education, and math. Math is important because food service professionals must be able to measure, multiply, divide, and work with fractions.

Other instruction occurs once service members complete basic training. Job training consists of nine to sixteen weeks of classroom instruction and hands-on practice in food preparation. Basic coursework includes instruction in preparing and cooking various foods and pastries, storage of meats and poultry, food ordering, planning nutritional menus, and food service operations and management. Food service personnel are encouraged to take more advanced training in general culinary arts or in specialty areas such as baking, butchering, or dining-facility finance throughout their military career.

Certification and Licensing

The military does not require food service professionals to hold special licenses or certification. However, the advanced training they receive in the military can help them get certification from various civilian organizations. Obtaining such credentials helps service members earn promotion points, which can accelerate their eligibility for promotion. In addition, these credentials help veterans gain employment after leaving the military. Credentials include but are not limited to: Certified Food Manager and Certified Food Executive from the International Food Service Executives Association; Certified Culinary Chef, Certified Executive Pastry Chef, Certified Sous Chef, and Personal Certified Chef from the American Culinary Federation, Inc. Certifications as Pro Chef levels 1–3 are available from the Culinary Institute of America.

Volunteer Work and Internships

Young people interested in a career in the military can learn about military life by participating in Junior Reserve Officer Training Corps (Jr. ROTC) in high school. Participants receive fitness training, which helps prepare individuals for basic training, and course credit for participating. Jr. ROTC members may go on trips to military bases where, among other things, they can see food service specialists in action.

Individuals can also learn about working in food service by getting a part-time or summer job in the kitchen of a summer camp, restaurant, coffee shop, or other eatery. Volunteering to serve and/or cook meals in a shelter that feeds the needy is another way to find out more about working in food services. Planning meals and cooking and baking for family members and friends, too, can help aspiring food service specialists hone their skills.

Skills and Personality

Cooking and serving food can be physically taxing. Food service specialists have to lift large, heavy cookware and trays of food. They have to repeatedly bend and reach, and stand on their feet for long periods of time. Therefore, they should be physically strong and fit. They should also have good eye-hand coordination and excellent personal hygiene.

These service members must also have good time-management skills and be able to stay calm and work well under pressure. Meals must be prepared in a timely fashion. And, no matter what may go wrong in the kitchen, whether the kitchen is located on a military base, a submarine, or in a combat zone, the troops need to be fed.

US military personnel and guests enjoy a Thanksgiving meal at a foreign military base. Food service specialists prepare and serve meals on a daily basis and on special occasions for thousands of service members.

Preparing meals for dignitaries can also be stressful. Cooks and servers must be able to do their work without being intimidated or overwhelmed by the importance of the occasion or the guests.

Being people oriented and having good people skills is helpful, too. Food service specialists spend a lot of time interacting with the men and women they serve. Friendly servers who are concerned with customer satisfaction help lift morale and make the dining experience pleasant for everyone. Having good communication skills is essential, too. Food specialists must be able to communicate easily with each other and with the service members they care for. These individuals should be creative and enjoy cooking and food preparation. Although following recipes is an important part of the job, so too is creativity. Military cooks are encouraged to be creative in their work, to add spices and flavorings, to try new things, and to make food look as appealing as possible. Finally, like all military personnel, these specialists must be able to follow orders from higher ranking personnel.

Employers

All five branches of the military employ food service specialists and managers. These service members may serve on active duty or in the reserves. Food service specialists are also known as culinary specialists in the Navy.

Working Conditions

Military food service personnel work indoors in kitchens and mess halls on US military bases throughout the world. They also work in military hospitals, on ships, submarines, aircraft carriers, and in tents under field conditions. They may be assigned to combat zones. Some work in military cooking schools as instructors. Those specializing in butchery may work in refrigerated meat lockers. These professionals usually work as part of a team in close proximity to other culinary specialists.

Earnings

Military pay is standardized. It is based on a service member's rank or grade and time in the service. According to the DOD, as of 2013 the base salary for active-duty enlisted personnel ranged from $16,824 to $89,220. In addition, service members may qualify for extra pay or bonuses. For example, food service specialists working in a combat zone receive an additional $375 per month for hazardous duty. Those serving in a foreign country where living conditions are substantially below those of the United States qualify for hardship pay, which ranges anywhere from $50 to $150 per month depending on the location. Moreover, all service members receive multiple opportunities to travel as well as benefits that can add up to a significant amount. Benefits include thirty days of paid vacation per year, free medical and dental care, education benefits, and retirement benefits. The military also provides all active-duty members who live on base with housing and food. Service members living off base receive a food and housing allowance. The amount is based on the service member's rank, family size, and location.

Each branch of the military also offers enlistment bonuses, which vary depending on the military branch, whether the recruit chooses active duty or the reserves, the terms of enlistment, the specific career field, and the enlistee's education and qualifications. Bonuses range from about $2,000 to $40,000. In addition, food service professionals who reenlist when their military service is up may be eligible for a reenlistment bonus.

Opportunities for Advancement

All service members have many opportunities for advancement. Typically, service members receive a raise in pay each time they go up in grade or rank. On average, this occurs every two years. However, individuals can advance more rapidly depending on their years in the military, job performance, military training, ongoing education, promotion points, and civilian certifications. By taking college classes at the military's expense; opting for advanced military training in culinary skills, menu planning, nutrition, leadership and management, accounting, budgeting, and finance, among other subjects; and by gaining civilian certification, food service specialists can advance rapidly. Moreover, food service specialists who obtain a bachelor's degree while serving in the military can be promoted to food service managers, which entitles them to a significant pay raise. Food service managers are commissioned officers. They manage the cooking and serving of every meal both in mess halls and in officers' dining facilities. They are also responsible for maintaining sanitary and nutritional standards in all food service facilities. This includes setting standards for food storage and preparation, and making sure these standards are met. Determining staffing for dining halls, kitchens, and meat-cutting plants is another part of these officers' job.

Generally, food service specialists start out as cooks, working under the supervision of more experienced cooking personnel. With increased training and experience, they are promoted to chefs. Chefs plan and prepare menus and recipes under the supervision of food service managers. They also supervise cooks, help order supplies and food, and serve as instructors in military culinary school. Chefs can advance to food service supervisors. These professionals set food service standards and operating procedures, prepare reports, and plan budgets under the supervision of a commissioned officer. In addition, as food service specialists advance in rank, they may be assigned to larger kitchens or mess halls or to dining facilities for officers, dignitaries, and important government officials.

Upon leaving the military, food service specialists often find work as restaurant owners and managers, bakers, butchers, caterers, chefs, and banquet planners. They also are employed by hotels, hospitals, schools, and corporations that have dining facilities. To help veterans gain civilian employment, the Army, in conjunction with a number of private corporations, sponsors the PaYS program. Service members who opt to take part in the program are guaranteed interviews with participating private corporations upon leaving the military. For food service professionals these corporations include Kraft Foods, McDonald's, Santa Fe Cattle Company, and Grand Sierra Resort, among others.

What Is the Future Outlook for Food Service Specialists and Managers?

The military employs about twenty-eight thousand food service specialists. As these service members leave the military, new culinary professionals are needed to replace them. Moreover, the military has been making an effort to serve less pre-prepared food and more freshly made food, which translates to a need for more food service personnel.

Find Out More

America's Navy: "Food, Restaurant, and Lodging"
website: www.navy.com

This article on the official US Navy website provides information about a career as a Navy culinary specialist. It includes a job description, explanation of responsibilities, and information about training and advancement.

Go Coast Guard: "Food Service Specialist"
website: www.gocoastguard.com

This article on the official Coast Guard website provides information about what it is like to be a food service specialist in the Coast Guard.

Military Chefs.com
phone: (202) 465-5153
e-mail: admin@militarychefs.com
website: www.militarychefs.com

This website is dedicated to military chefs. It offers numerous video interviews with military chefs, military chef news, information about military cooking competitions, and many helpful links.

US Military.com
website: www.usmilitary.com

This website provides a wealth of information about the five branches of the military and the various careers in each branch, including an article on US Navy cooks. In addition, there is information about the ASVAB test, preparing for basic training, videos, links, and related news.

Intelligence Specialist

What Does an Intelligence Specialist Do?

Intelligence specialists or analysts gather information, known as intelligence, from a multitude of sources. Using aerial photographs, advanced computer systems, electronic surveillance equipment, satellites, and human intelligence, intelligence specialists collect, interpret, and disseminate information about the location, capabilities, and tactics of enemy forces. All five branches of the military depend upon this information to support combat operations and the safety of Americans.

In a typical day intelligence specialists study images of foreign bases, airfields, missile sites, and sea areas that might harbor foreign ships or submarines. These pictures may have been taken by pilots, satellites, or unmanned aircraft known as drones. The pictures are sent as digital images via computer to these specialists who are trained to analyze each image pixel by pixel. They look beyond the obvious—isolating patterns, shadows, and shapes that may be hidden weapons, vehicles, temporary structures, or hostile forces. Then they prepare reports, graphs, charts, maps, and oral communications based on the intelligence they have gathered. Their reports often include recommendations for targets for

At a Glance:
Intelligence Specialist

Minimum Educational Requirements
High school diploma

Personal Qualities
Interest in maps and charts; comfortable with technology

Certification and Licensing
Top secret security clearance

Working Conditions
In offices on land, ships, or field tents

Salary Range
Basic pay from about $16,824 to $89,220

Number of Jobs
As of 2013 about 26,000

Future Job Outlook
Good

military missions. In an article on the Careers in the Military website, army intelligence specialist Melissa Taylor explains: "My favorite job was as a Targeting Analyst while deployed in support of Operation Iraqi Freedom. It was our job to identify, develop and recommend targets (individuals, groups, or areas). In this role, I had the opportunity to work with different intelligence disciplines, other government agencies, Special Operations Forces, and Navy Seals."

Intelligence personnel also monitor real-time video feeds taken by drones and report on what they see via text messages to troops in the field. During the US war in Iraq, which began in 2003, intelligence specialist Air Force master sergeant Mary Bechdel detected concealed enemy forces by studying a video feed. The hostile forces intended to launch a surprise attack on an approaching military convoy. Acting quickly, Bechdel called for air support to protect the convoy. Her rapid action saved many lives. At other times Bechdel reported hundreds of potential improvised explosive devices, which she detected by studying still and video images.

Intelligence specialists also derive information by monitoring enemy communications. They use high-tech surveillance equipment to intercept enemy radio and phone communications, enemy e-mails, text messages, tweets, and other online chatter. It is their job to decipher, analyze, and report on such communications. Often this involves translating the data from a foreign language to English or breaking enemy codes.

Although many intelligence specialists work mainly with data, some come in direct contact with enemy combatants and foreign communities. Using foreign language skills, they may be involved with interviewing or interrogating individuals who are considered a threat to national security. Sometimes they gather information out in the field. For instance, during the Iraq War, intelligence specialists dressed to look like native Iraqis, mingled with the locals, and eavesdropped on their conversations. In this way they gathered intelligence that helped protect fellow service members.

The military divides intelligence specialists into three general groups: imagery intelligence (IMINT), signals intelligence (SIGINT), and human intelligence (HUMINT). Service members who specialize in imagery intelligence work with visual images such as photographs and video feeds. Those who specialize in signals intelligence work with enemy communications such as radio messages and e-mails. Human intelligence specialists gather information person-to-person. This specialty is the most dangerous.

How Do You Become an Intelligence Specialist?

Education

Intelligence specialists are enlisted service members. As such, they are required to be high school graduates. To prepare for a career as an intelligence specialist, high school students should take classes that require critical thinking. These include classes in math, science, social studies, and world history. Other beneficial classes include geography and computer technology. Learning a foreign language is also important for advancing in this career.

Once service members have successfully gone through basic training, the military provides intelligence specialists with classroom training and simulated field training in information gathering. Training takes from nine to twenty-four weeks. Coursework includes instruction in using computer technology and aerial, radar, and satellite imagery. It also covers analyzing aerial photographs and communication data. Instruction in storing and retrieving intelligence data and preparing reports, maps, graphs, and charts is also part of the curriculum. Other training occurs on the job and through advanced courses. The latter may include classes in foreign languages and cultures. For example, the Defense Language Institute Foreign Language Center in Monterey, California, offers intelligence specialists and other service members the opportunity to learn up to twenty-three different languages in an immersive environment. Training includes intensive language instruction coupled with instruction in the history and culture of the associated countries. Training lasts about two years. Upon completion of the coursework service members receive an associate's degree.

Certification and Licensing

Military intelligence specialists are not required to have any specific certificates or licenses. They must, however, have top secret security clearance. It is the highest level of security clearance possible. Gaining top secret security clearance indicates that the military certifies the individual is loyal to the United States and able to be trusted with sensitive information that could cause great damage to the nation if it is leaked. Gaining top secret security clearance is difficult. Applicants must be US citizens. They must not have a police record. And they must pass an intensive background check and personal interview, which include a review of their personal, legal, and financial history. The applicant's family, too, must pass a background check and must be US citizens. In addition, aspiring intelligence specialists' friends, neighbors, former employers, and coworkers are interviewed and questioned about the applicant's trustworthiness.

Once a service member becomes an intelligence specialist, through ongoing military training he or she can gain credentials or certification from various federal and private agencies at the military's expense. Obtaining such credentials helps service members earn promotion points that may help them gain employment when they return to civilian life. These credentials include counterterrorism specialist certification, homeland security certification, mapping scientist certification, remote sensing technologist certification, and Microsoft applications specialist certification, among others.

Volunteer Work and Internships

Young people interested in a career as an intelligence specialist can learn about what military life is like by participating in Junior Reserve Officer Training Corps (Jr. ROTC) in high school. Participation helps keep individuals physically fit, which can help recruits get through basic training more easily. In addition to fitness training Jr. ROTC members receive course credit for participating in activities such as map reading and field trips to military bases.

Skills and Personality

Intelligence specialists should be patient, focused, and detail oriented. It takes time and intense concentration to analyze data thoroughly, discover patterns and hidden details, and prepare accurate maps, graphs, and charts. The job also requires logic, critical thinking skills, and good problem-solving skills. Indeed, curious, investigative individuals who enjoy using knowledge to solve problems are drawn to this profession.

Physically, these professionals need good eyesight with normal color vision, since some specialties work with color-coded maps. Imagery analysts must also have good depth perception. Mentally and emotionally, intelligence specialists should be strong and able to handle stress. Analyzing intelligence is a demanding job. Information is always coming in. Specialists must stay on top of the situation. They are under intense pressure to work quickly without sacrificing accuracy. Multiple lives depend on their work.

Intelligence specialists also need good communication skills. Since they are responsible for preparing reports and giving oral briefings to commanders and troops, they should be able to speak and write clearly. They must be comfortable using computers and other technology and have good key-board skills. And since their work is classified, they must be able to keep secrets. This includes not speaking about their work with their families and friends. In addition, because the work of intelligence specialists is often a team effort, they should be able to work with and get along well with others and take orders from intelligence officers without any problems.

On the Job

Employers

All five branches of the military employ intelligence specialists. These service members may serve on active duty or in the reserves.

Working Conditions

Imagery, signal, and human intelligence specialists work in offices on military bases and in intelligence production centers in the United States and overseas. They also work aboard ships, aircraft carriers, submarines, in field tents, and with aircraft squadrons. Specialists in human intelligence often work covertly in foreign countries. Since information gathering does not stop, these service members work in shifts. Shift work includes working days, nights, holidays, and weekends. In addition, they are on call should an emergency arise.

Earnings

Military pay is standardized. It is based on a service member's rank or grade and time in the service. According to the DOD, as of 2013 the base salary for active-duty enlisted service members ranged from $16,824 to $89,220. Service members with specific skills may qualify for additional special pay. For instance, human intelligence specialists may receive an additional $375 per month for hazardous duty. Intelligence specialists who are fluent in certain foreign languages such as Arabic or Chinese receive an additional $200 per month. Moreover, all service members receive multiple opportunities to travel as well as paid benefits that can add up to a significant amount. Benefits include thirty days of paid vacation per year, free medical and dental care, education benefits, and retirement benefits. The military also provides all active-duty members who live on base with housing and food. Personnel living off base receive a food and housing allowance. The amount is based on the service member's rank, family size, and location.

In addition, each branch of the military offers enlistment bonuses, which vary depending on the military branch, whether the recruit chooses active duty or the reserves, the terms of enlistment, the military career, and the enlistee's education and qualifications. For instance, enlistees fluent in a foreign language can earn a $5,000 cash bonus depending on the language.

Moreover, because this job specialty is considered a critical area by the military, if an intelligence specialist chooses to remain on active duty for an additional year after finishing his or her terms of enlistment, that individual can receive a retention bonus. Those who reenlist after completing their tour of duty are eligible for a lucrative reenlistment bonus. The amount of either bonus depends on the service member's experience, training, and special skills.

Opportunities for Advancement

Typically, service members receive a raise in pay each time they go up in grade or rank. This usually occurs every two years. However, individuals can advance more rapidly based on their experience, job performance, training, ongoing education, and civilian certifications, among other things. Therefore, as intelligence specialists receive different types of training they can earn pay increases as well as promotions. Intelligence specialists can also earn an associate's or bachelor's degree through distance-learning programs while serving in the military. These programs allow military personnel to earn college credit based on their military occupational specialty and experience. For instance, based on their military experience, naval intelligence specialists can earn up to thirty-nine credit hours toward a bachelor's degree in computer studies, digital media and web technology, or management studies. Once specialists earn a bachelor's degree they can advance to commissioned officer.

Upon leaving the military, intelligence specialists often find managerial jobs working for federal government agencies such as the Central Intelligence Agency, the National Security Administration, and Homeland Security. Moreover, because top secret security clearances are difficult to obtain, individuals who held top secret security clearance are highly sought in the private sector. Their analytical, organizational, and computer skills also make these professionals valuable civilian employees.

What Is the Future Outlook for Intelligence Specialists?

The military has about twenty-six thousand intelligence specialists. New personnel are needed each year to replace personnel returning to civilian life. In addition, the ongoing threat of global terrorism has increased the demand for intelligence specialists, especially those fluent in Middle Eastern languages and knowledgeable about Middle Eastern cultures.

Find Out More

America's Navy: "Intelligence Specialist"
website: www.navy.com

The official website of the US Navy provides information about a career as a Navy intelligence specialist. It includes a job description, information about qualifications, training, advancement, and pay.

Careers in the Military: "Intelligence Specialist"
website: www.careersinthemilitary.com

This DOD website provides information on every branch of the military and military career. The Intelligence Specialist page gives information on the profession and provides a link to an interview with an intelligence specialist.

Go Army: "Intelligence Analyst"
website: www.goarmy.com

The official website of the US Army offers information about careers in the Army. The "Intelligence Analyst" page provides information about this career, including information about the job, helpful skills, qualification, and training.

Today's Military: "Intelligence Careers"
website: www.todaysmilitary.com

This US government website offers a wealth of information about joining the military, military life, and different military careers. The section on intelligence careers provides information about intelligence specialist jobs, related civilian careers, interviews with service members, videos, and links.

Law Enforcement and Security Specialist

The US military has its own police force. They are known as military police (MPs), masters-at-arms, maritime enforcement specialists, or security force specialists, depending on the branch of the service. These professionals enforce military law on military bases, in coastal waters, and in combat zones. They also deal with crimes that occur outside of military property involving military personnel and property. Like civilian law enforcement professionals, they investigate crimes, enforce traffic regulations, respond to emergencies, and operate and guard military prisons. In addition, they help protect service members and base security by guarding access points on bases and manning entrance and exit checkpoints.

On a typical day these specialists may gather evidence in a case involving the theft of military property, conduct a surveillance operation, or intervene in

At a Glance:

Law Enforcement and Security Specialist

Minimum Educational Requirements
High school diploma

Personal Qualities
Able to stay calm under pressure; physically fit

Certification and Licensing
Secret security clearance; driver's license

Working Conditions
Indoors and outdoors

Salary Range
Basic pay from about $16,824 to $89,220

Number of Jobs
As of 2013 about 30,000

Future Job Outlook
Good

41

a domestic dispute. They may investigate activities related to treason, espionage, or terrorism. Or they may apprehend, detain, and question a crime suspect, interview witnesses, and secure a crime scene. They also may provide protective service to high-ranking officers or important dignitaries.

Those serving in the Navy and Coast Guard often patrol on water. Coast Guard maritime enforcement specialists are responsible for the security and safety of US ports. Among other tasks, Navy security personnel provide protective service for Navy ships visiting foreign ports and provide lead and rear security for motor convoys.

For those law enforcement specialists stationed in a combat zone, other daily activities may include patrolling and guarding supply and frequently traveled routes and locating and defusing concealed improvised explosive devices (IEDs). Some of these specialists also provide security for aircraft flying in and out of hostile territories. In this role they guard air crews and aircraft from enemy attacks.

These professionals can serve as general law enforcement officers or, with advanced training, they can specialize. One such specialty is dog handler. These men and women work with canine partners trained in explosive detection. They often work in combat zones. Some dog handlers work with Special Forces teams. Others work in direct support of the president of the United States. They guard and check for explosives in and around aircraft used to transport the president. As Army dog handler Sergeant Danny Roger explains on the Go Army website: "My dog, Igor, is specially trained in explosives. We get these dogs when they're puppies and by the time that they are one and a half to two years old, they can save millions of lives."

Criminal investigation agents, known as criminal investigation command (CIC) or criminal investigation service (CIS) agents, depending on the military branch, are other specialists. They investigate major felony crimes, such as murders, involving the military. They work closely with civilian law enforcement agencies and with federal intelligence agencies. These agents can further specialize in the fields of polygraph operations and analysis, forensics, computer crimes, economic crimes, or terrorism. Those in the Coast Guard also deal with drug trafficking, illegal immigration, and environmental crimes occurring in coastal waters. Navy CIS agents are involved in deterring piracy on the high seas. Since 2008, CIS agents have investigated dozens of piracy cases, most of which occurred in African waters. Agents have interrogated piracy suspects awaiting trial in the United States and Kenya and have processed piracy crime scenes.

How Do You Become a Law Enforcement and Security Specialist?

Education

Law enforcement and security specialists are enlisted personnel. As such, they are required to be high school graduates. To prepare for this job in high school, young people should take classes in psychology, government, physical education, English, and speech.

Once aspiring military police officers have successfully gone through basic training, the military provides them with five to twelve weeks of classroom instruction in the career. Coursework includes instruction in military and civil law, evidence-gathering procedures, report writing, and crime-scene investigations. Traffic and crowd control, prisoner control, use of firearms, hand-to-hand defense tactics, crime photography, and terrorism threat response procedures are also covered.

Certification and Licensing

These professionals must have a valid driver's license. No other license or certification is required for the job. However, to serve as military police, service members must have either confidential or secret security clearance, depending on the specialty and branch of the military. To obtain either security clearance, individuals must pass a background check. Receiving a security clearance indicates that the military has established that the individual is loyal to the United States and will not disclose confidential information.

While serving in the military, law enforcement and security specialists can gain certification from various federal and private agencies at the military's expense. Obtaining such credentials helps service members earn promotion points, which can increase their chances of promotion. They also help veterans find civilian employment. These credentials include but are not limited to background investigation certification, certified accident investigator, certified counterterrorism specialist, advanced law enforcement planner, certified crime scene analyst, and certified protection professional. Military training may also help these professionals gain state licensure as a polygraph examiner, accident reconstruction specialist, and/or private investigator.

Volunteer Work and Internships

Young people interested in a career in military law enforcement can learn about what military life is like by participating in Junior Reserve Officer Training Corps (Jr. ROTC) in high school. Participation helps keep individuals physically fit. In addition, Jr. ROTC members receive course credit for participating.

Prospective military police officers can also learn more about police work by shadowing a civilian law enforcement officer. Many police departments sponsor ride-along programs, which allow young people to learn more about the profession by riding along with an officer in a police cruiser.

In addition, the Naval Criminal Investigative Service offers unpaid internships to civilian college students at their national headquarters in Quantico, Virginia, and in their field offices. These internships help prepare college graduates for careers as commissioned military security forces officers.

Skills and Personality

Law enforcement and security specialists must be physically fit. Foot-patrolling, chasing and subduing criminals, and working outdoors in bad weather are all part of the job. These activities require physical strength and stamina. The job also requires courage. These service members perform potentially dangerous work on a daily basis. Suspects trained in the use of firearms can become violent at any time. Military police must be willing to face danger. And they must be willing to risk their own safety in order to keep others safe.

Other physical requirements include normal hearing, normal color vision, and vision correctable to 20/20. Clear speaking ability is also needed. Military police must be able to communicate effectively with bystanders, suspects, and lawyers, among other personnel. And because of the authority these men and women hold over other service members, the military holds these professionals to a high level of accountability. No history of mental illness, emotional instability, drug abuse, alcoholism, or criminal history is allowed for those in this career. The military feels that a past history of these conditions can impact a law enforcement specialist's ability to do the job.

In addition to being physically strong, these law enforcement experts must also be emotionally strong and stable. They should be able to stay calm under pressure. It is not unusual for emotionally distraught individuals to scream at, threaten, or insult these officers. To do their job effectively, law enforcement specialists cannot take this treatment personally. They must be patient, polite, and in control of their temper. Being detail oriented is also important. It keeps investigators from missing important clues in a case. Good problem-solving skills, too, are essential in solving cases.

On the Job

Employers

These service members are employed by all five branches of the military. They can serve on active duty or in the reserves.

Working Conditions

Military security forces work indoors and outdoors in all types of weather and terrain. They are often involved in potentially dangerous situations. They work anywhere in the world where there is a US military presence. This includes military bases and shore stations, aboard ships and aircraft carriers, in US ports, in military prisons, and in combat zones. They generally work twelve-hour shifts, consisting of two days on followed by two days off. Depending on their schedule, they may work weekends and holidays. They usually work in teams or with a partner.

Earnings

Military pay is standardized. It is based on a service member's rank or grade and years in the service. According to the DOD, as of 2013 the base salary for active-duty enlisted service members ranged from $16,824 to $89,220. Service members with specific skills may qualify for additional pay. For instance, dog handlers are paid an additional $2,000 per year. All personnel serving in a combat zone receive an additional $375 per month for hazardous duty. Moreover, all service members receive multiple opportunities to travel as well as benefits that can add up to a significant amount. Benefits include thirty days of paid vacation per year, free medical and dental care, education benefits, and retirement benefits. The military also provides all active-duty members who live on base with housing and food. Service members living off base receive a food and housing allowance. The amount is based on the service member's rank, family size, and location.

In addition, each branch of the military offers enlistment bonuses, which vary depending on the military branch, whether the recruit chooses active duty or the reserves, the terms of enlistment, the military career, and the enlistee's education and qualifications. Moreover, CID and CIS agents, dog handlers, and military police who reenlist after completing their tour of duty are eligible for a reenlistment bonus ranging up to $15,000, depending on the service member's experience and training and the terms of reenlistment.

Opportunities for Advancement

The military provides its members many opportunities for advancement. Each time service members go up in rank they receive a raise in pay. Typically, this occurs every two years. However, individuals can advance more rapidly based on their job performance, training, ongoing education, civilian certification, and promotion points, among other things.

Inexperienced law enforcement specialists start out as military police officers. They can advance to squad leaders, who manage a squad of military police, and then to law enforcement supervisors or superintendents, who manage all military police members on large bases. They can also branch out into investigative specialties. Law enforcement specialists can earn an associate's or bachelor's degree in criminology at the military's expense by taking coursework on base, through a distance-learning program, or at a nearby college. Once specialists earn a bachelor's degree, they can advance to commissioned military law enforcement officers.

Upon leaving the military these professionals often are employed by metropolitan, state, and federal law enforcement agencies or as security personnel for large corporations. Moreover, because obtaining confidential or secret security clearance is difficult, individuals who have held security clearance are highly sought after in the private sector.

What Is the Future Outlook for Law Enforcement and Security Specialists?

The military employs about thirty thousand law enforcement and security specialists. As experienced specialists leave the service, new personnel are needed to fill these positions. Moreover, there is an increasing demand in all branches of the service for security forces specializing in computer or cybercrimes.

Find Out More

Naval Criminal Investigative Service (NCIS)
27130 Telegraph Rd.
Quantico, VA 22134
phone: (877) 579-3648
website: www.ncis.mil

This is the official website of NCIS. It provides information about NCIS, careers in NCIS, and profiles of NCIS agents.

Navy Personnel Command: "Master-at-Arms"
5720 Integrity Dr.
Millington, TN 38055

phone: (866) 827–5672
website: www.public.navy.mil

This website run by the US Navy offers information on different careers in the Navy. The "Master-at-Arms" page provides information about this job.

US Air Force: "Security Forces Specialist"
website: www.airforce.com

The official website of the US Air Force offers information about various careers in this branch of the military. The "Security Forces Specialist" page provides information about this career.

US Army Criminal Investigations Command
Russell Knox Bldg.
27130 Telegraph Rd.
Quantico, VA 22134
phone: (571) 305-4009
website: www.cid.army.mil

The official website of the Army CID offers information about the job, becoming a CID team member, training, and ongoing investigations worldwide.

Medic

What Does a Medic Do?

In places where physicians are not immediately available, such as on a battlefield, medics provide emergency medical treatment to injured troops. They do everything possible to stabilize wounded warriors until they get to hospitals or other treatment facilities. They also assist physicians and nurses in military hospitals or shipboard sick bays. Some serve on independent duty caring for the health needs of crews on submarines or isolated duty stations. They also train service members in first aid, trauma care, and preventive medicine. These health care professionals serve in the Army, Air Force, Navy, and Coast Guard. The Marines do not have medics. Instead, every Marine Corps unit has a Navy hospital corpsman with them.

Officially known as medical service technicians in the Army, hospital corpsmen in the Navy, aerospace medical service specialists in the Air Force, health service technicians in the Coast Guard, and nicknamed "medics" or "docs," these individuals have a lot of responsibility. Although no two days are the same in this career, in a typical day these medical professionals may be found accompanying patrols into enemy territory, providing

At a Glance:

Medic

Minimum Educational Requirements
High school diploma

Personal Qualities
Calm under pressure; desire to help others

Certification and Licensing
None

Working Conditions
Indoors and outdoors

Salary Range
Basic pay from about $16,824 to $89,220

Number of Jobs
As of 2013 about 27,000

Future Job Outlook
Good

49

fire to help subdue hostile forces, and treating wounded service members on the battlefield. Or they may work as part of a helicopter medevac squad, evacuating, treating, and transporting wounded troops from combat zones.

Medics can also be found assisting physicians and nurses in the prevention and treatment of diseases and injuries in field hospitals, in large military hospitals and health clinics, and aboard ships. A workday for medics in these medical facilities may include interviewing patients and checking their vital signs, changing bandages, delivering immunizations, and taking blood samples. It may also include suturing wounds, applying casts, administering medication, and taking and processing X-rays. Preparing operating-room equipment and supplies, readying patients for surgery, and serving as an operating-room assistant are other aspects of a typical workday. A workday for a corpsman at an isolated duty station or on a submarine includes many of the same duties. However, these docs operate without the assistance of a physician or nurse.

When these health care professionals are not administering direct care, they may be training military personnel in first aid, maintaining patients' medical records, and participating in training scenarios that prepare service members for deployment. These men and women are also instrumental in setting up field hospitals.

How Do You Become a Medic?

Education

Medics are enlisted personnel. As such, they are required to be a high school graduate. To prepare for this career, high school students should take classes in health, biology, chemistry, psychology, and physical education. Once prospective medics in all branches of the military have completed basic training, they are assigned to Fort Sam Houston in Texas where they receive sixteen to fifty-four weeks of classroom and hands-on instruction. Coursework includes instruction in first aid, emergency medicine techniques, trauma care, patient care, working with surgical equipment, and preparing a plaster cast. Assembling and operating medical machinery such as oxygen-delivery equipment is also learned. So, too, are maintaining medical records, taking and processing X-rays, and performing laboratory tests such as drawing blood. After completing classroom instruction, new medics receive on-the-job training under the supervision of experienced medics and other health care professionals.

With more advanced training, these service members can choose to specialize in a particular area. Specialties include radiology, dialysis, cardiovascular care, respiratory medicine, search-and-rescue medical technician, preventive medicine specialist, submarine force independent duty, and field medical technician, to name a few. There are so many specialty areas open to medics that it is the most diverse enlisted medical field in the service.

Certification and Licensing

Service members can enter this career without any previous licenses or certification. The training they receive in the military combined with on-the-job experience makes it possible for them to gain a wide range of certifications from various health care organizations at the military's expense. Obtaining such credentials helps service members earn promotion points that may accelerate their promotions as well as help veterans find civilian employment. These credentials include both clinical care and nonclinical care certificates. Clinical care certificates include emergency medical technician, first responder, certified EKG technician, certified patient care technician, and national certified phlebotomy technician. Nonclinical certificates include but are not limited to disaster preparedness, homeland security, medical administrative assistant, and billing and coding.

Volunteer Work and Internships

In many respects a medic's job is similar to that of an emergency medical technician (EMT). One way to learn more about the job is by shadowing an EMT. Some volunteer rescue services, fire departments, and ambulance services let young people ride along on emergency calls. Joining a volunteer fire department or other rescue organization or working as a lifeguard are other ways to test how well suited an individual may be for this career. These jobs put aspiring medics in a position of responsibility for taking care of others, which is a large part of what a medic does. Volunteering in a hospital or nursing home is also helpful. Doing so allows individuals to get more experience in a health care setting.

Participating in Junior Reserve Officer Training Corps (Jr. ROTC) in high school is beneficial, too. It gives young people the chance to learn about military life. Participation helps individuals become physically fit. In addition, Jr. ROTC members receive course credit for participating.

Skills and Personality

Being a medic is physically demanding. These medical professionals are on their feet for long periods of time. They repeatedly bend, kneel, and reach. They lift and carry wounded patients over all types of terrain. They must be physically strong and fit to do their job. In fact, members of helicopter evacuation squads must pass a special physical exam to qualify for the job.

These men and women should be emotionally strong, too. Medics are confronted by traumatic situations on a daily basis. Even with the best of care, troops die or are hurt so badly that their lives are changed forever. Although medics must be compassionate and have a strong desire to help others, in order to maintain their mental health and do their job well they need to be able to accept these situations without becoming overwhelmed. Since corpsmen often live, work, and develop close relationships with the service members they care for, maintaining emotional distance can be quite challenging.

Moreover, since these professionals often work under combat conditions, they must be able to stay calm under pressure. They also should be brave and selfless. Medics often face hostile fire while treating battlefield casualties. In many instances they have to risk their own safety in order to do their job. If they cannot do this, or if they panic, lives may be lost—including their own.

Being able to act independently and having excellent problem-solving skills are also essential. In combat situations, the medic is usually the only health care professional on the scene. It is up to the medic to make medical decisions without the guidance of other health care professionals. Medics must be able to solve problems, make rapid decisions, and act quickly during a crisis situation.

At the same time, medics must be able to work as part of a team. They are responsible for the health of every member of their unit. In military hospitals and clinics they take orders from physicians and nurses. Being able to get along with others is vital to their success

On the Job

Employers

Medics are employed by the Army, Navy, Air Force, and Coast Guard. They serve as active military and in the reserves.

Working Conditions

These health care professionals serve indoors and outdoors under a wide range of working conditions. They work in clean, climate-controlled US military hospitals. They also work in health clinics on military bases, on ships, aircraft carriers, submarines, with air squadrons, in field hospitals, and as part of Special Forces units. Female medics are not assigned to submarines, the fleet Marine force, Special Forces units, or as combat medics. However, they may work in field hospitals in hostile territory.

Medics who work in military hospitals and health clinics usually work rotating twelve-hour shifts with three or four days off per week. Depending on the shift, they may work nights, weekends, and holidays, and they are on call.

Combat medics and corpsmen are on call seven days a week, day and night. When the unit they are assigned to is sent on patrol, they accompany the unit into battle. Like all combat service members, they are armed and participate in combat duties. They can be deployed anywhere in the world. They mainly work outdoors in dangerous situations.

Earnings

Military pay is standardized. It is based on a service member's rank or grade and time in the service. According to the DOD, as of 2013 the base salary for active-duty enlisted personnel ranged from $16,824 to $89,220. All troops serving in a combat zone receive an additional $375 per month for hazardous duty. Moreover, all service members receive multiple opportunities to travel as well as benefits that can add up to a significant amount. Benefits include thirty days of paid vacation per year, free medical and dental care, education benefits, and retirement benefits. The military also provides all active-duty members who live on base with housing and food. Service members living off base receive a food and housing allowance based on the service member's rank, family size, and location. In addition, each branch of the military offers monetary enlistment and reenlistment bonuses, which vary depending on the military branch, whether the individual chooses active duty or the reserves, his or her education and qualifications, and the terms of enlistment/reenlistment. For example, the Navy offers hospital corpsmen who reenlist up to $60,000.

Opportunities for Advancement

The military provides its members many opportunities for advancement. Each time service members go up in rank they receive a raise in pay. Typically, this occurs every two years. Individuals can advance more rapidly based on their job performance, training, ongoing education, civilian certification, and promotion points, among other things. By taking coursework on base, at a nearby college, or through a distance-learning program, medics can earn an associate's or bachelor's degree qualifying them to be a nurse, paramedic, or physician's assistant at the military's expense. Upon leaving the military these men and women often find employment with ambulance services and in hospitals and other health care facilities.

What Is the Future Outlook for Medics?

The military has about twenty-seven thousand medics. New personnel are needed each year to replace personnel returning to civilian life. Moreover, since wounded service members returning from Afghanistan and Iraq must be cared for, and keeping troops healthy is top priority, the need for these health care professionals should continue to grow.

Find Out More

America's Navy: "Medical Support Jobs"
website: www.navy.com

This article on the official website of the US Navy provides information about a career as a hospital corpsman including a job description, list of responsibilities, and data on training and advancement. There are links to information about joining the Navy.

Corpsman.com
website: www.corpsman.com

This is a website for all enlisted medical personnel. It offers recruiting information, historical information, a forum, and news.

Go Army: "Health Care Specialist"
website: www.goarmy.com

This article gives information about a career as an Army medic. It is part of the official US Army website, which also gives information about the Army and enlisting.

US Air Force: "Aerospace Medical Service"
website: www.airforce.com

This article on the official US Air Force website provides information about a career as an Air Force medic with links to related Air Force careers and general information about the Air Force.

Pilot

Airplanes and helicopters are an essential part of the US military. In the hands of military pilots, these aircraft are used to transport troops and equipment, execute combat missions, carry out rescue operations, and gather intelligence. In addition, most military pilots are commissioned officers with all the related responsibilities.

In a typical day a pilot may attend a mission briefing, study flight plans, maps, and mission details, and confer with air traffic controllers. Mission briefings can last for hours, especially if the mission involves an incursion into hostile territory. As Air Force pilot Cameron Schaefer explains in an interview on The Art of Manliness website, "I think a lot of people think we just hop in the jet and go joyriding, not realizing how scripted each mission is and how much planning is involved. Not to say that it isn't fun, but there is always a mission whether it's operational or simply training." Missions may involve dropping bombs on enemy targets, engaging in aerial warfare with enemy aircraft, transporting fuel to other aircraft for mid-air refueling, or flying close to the ocean's surface in search of underwater mines or enemy submarines, among other things.

At a Glance:
Pilot

Minimum Educational Requirements
Bachelor's degree

Personal Qualities
Quick reflexes; calm under pressure

Certification and Licensing
None

Working Conditions
On airbases and in aircraft

Salary Range
Base annual salary from $33,732 to $179,700

Number of Jobs
As of 2013 about 16,000 airplane pilots and 6,500 helicopter pilots

Future Job Outlook
Good

Before taking off on a mission pilots make sure the aircraft's controls and flight deck equipment are in working order. Once on a mission, these men and women fly the aircraft. This involves directing the aircraft's course using radar, monitoring cockpit instruments, and adjusting the controls. At the same time they may also perform combat maneuvers, take reconnaissance photos, or track enemy positions. They may also operate bombardier systems, transport valuable equipment and personnel, or participate in search-and-rescue operations. Their work is often dangerous, which is why the motto "That others may live," is the motto of Air Force rescue pilots. They are men and women who fly into enemy territory to rescue injured service members.

Rescue pilots are one of a number of pilot specialties. Military aviators may be generalists, or they may specialize in a specific duty and a specific aircraft. Specialties include bomber pilot, fighter pilot, and special operations pilot. Trainer pilot, tanker pilot, experimental test pilot, reconnaissance/surveillance pilot, and helicopter pilot are other specialties. Most pilots usually specialize in particular aircraft, too. For example, bomber pilots commonly specialize in piloting a B-52.

Both male and female service members can be pilots. However, because direct combat missions are currently limited to men, female service members do not yet have the option of pursuing aviation combat specialties such as bomber, fighter, or special operations pilot.

How Do You Become a Pilot?

Education

All Air Force, Navy, Marine, and Coast Guard pilots are commissioned officers. As such, they are required to have a minimum of a bachelor's degree and have successfully completed officer's training. Prospective officers can attend officer's training school as part of their military training, or they can become commissioned officers by attending one of the military service academies or by completing ROTC training in a civilian college.

Army pilots are the only group who do not have to hold a bachelor's degree. The Army has a unique program known as "from high school to flight school," which allows high school graduates to become pilots.

Becoming a pilot through this program is extremely competitive. Preference is given to recruits with an associate's degree or two years of college credit, a private pilot's license, proven leadership ability, and a high score on the Army's Flight Aptitude Test. Army pilots without a college degree receive the ranking of warrant officer. A warrant officer is a technical expert, whose pay and military ranking is slightly lower than that of a fully commissioned officer.

No matter what branch of the service a prospective pilot is interested in joining, to prepare for a career as an aviator high school students should take classes in physical education, math, computer science, speech, and physics. In college aspiring pilots can select any major. Coursework in physics, math, computer science, geography, and aeronautical engineering are helpful.

Comprehensive flying instruction occurs in the military. Acceptance to flight school is competitive. Typically, there are more applicants than pilot openings. Since it costs about $1 million to train a pilot, the military is highly selective in filling flight school slots. Applicants must pass a very demanding physical exam (beyond the physical exam required to enlist). In addition, they must exhibit outstanding character and leadership traits. Although pilots can come from a civilian background, preference is given to graduates of the service academies and to applicants who have successfully completed ROTC.

Recruits who are accepted into flight school undergo about two years of demanding training. Ten- to twelve-hour days are the norm. Instruction includes classroom studies, simulator flight training, and actual flight experience. Classroom lessons cover coursework in aerodynamics, emergency procedures, reading and drawing flight maps, and aircraft systems, among other topics.

Once aspiring aviators complete primary classroom training, instruction focuses on specialty areas. Competition for certain specialties, such as fighter pilot, can be intense. Trainees are ranked based on their abilities and performance in the classroom, then assigned a career specialty. Those ranking highest are most likely to be trained as fighter pilots.

Simulator and flight training is specific to each recruit's assigned specialty. For instance, helicopter pilot trainees spend time in a spinning chair that simulates the spinning movement of a helicopter. Total actual in-flight training ranges from 108 to 228 hours, and total simulator training ranges from 12 to 109 hours. Flight instructors evaluate trainees during actual and virtual flights. Inadequate performance can lead to a trainee being removed from the program. One Air Force pilot reports that out of the twenty-nine individuals he trained with, only seventeen finished the program.

Certification and Licensing

Military aviators do not need any type of license or certification for this job. Pilots earn their "wings" by successfully completing military flight school. They can use their military flight training and flying experience to help them get a civilian flight instructor license, a private or commercial pilot license, and/or a commercial rotocraft (helicopter) license. Since civilian flight training is quite expensive, this is a significant benefit for veterans who seek civilian flying careers. Many pilots employed by commercial airlines and helicopter companies received their flight training in the military.

Volunteer Work and Internships

To prepare for a career as a pilot young people between the ages of twelve to nineteen can become cadets in the Civil Air Patrol (CAP), a volunteer civilian organization associated with the Air Force. Cadets have the opportunity to go on flights in CAP airplanes, and they can compete for scholarships that help pay for private flight instruction. Moreover, the service academies look favorably on CAP cadet applicants. In fact, former CAP cadets comprise about 10 percent of US Air Force Academy students.

Participating in Junior Reserve Officer Training Corps (Jr. ROTC) in high school and ROTC in college is beneficial too. Participation gives young people the chance to learn about military life and helps individuals become physically fit. In addition, Jr. ROTC and ROTC members receive course credit for participating. College ROTC members are also given the opportunity to participate in summer training that often includes airborne training.

Other experiences can help aspiring pilots reach their goal, too. Using computer software such as Microsoft Flight Simulator is a good way to develop skills needed to fly a plane.

Skills and Personality

Pilots must be physically fit. Flights can last hours, and cockpit temperatures can be uncomfortable. Pilots must have good stamina to successfully complete a mission. Fighter pilots and test pilots who fly at high speeds face powerful G-forces (the force of Earth's gravity pulling down on an object) and must be physically strong to withstand the force. Medical requirements for the job are strict. Pilots must have 20/20 vision, correctable with eyeglasses; normal depth perception; normal night vision; and normal color vision. They must also have good hearing, normal blood pressure and heart rate, and be free of any physical handicaps that could affect their ability to do their job. Quick reflexes, excellent eye-hand coordination, and good spatial perception are also needed.

In addition to physical requirements, the military looks for certain personal characteristics in pilot candidates. These traits include a high need to achieve, self-discipline, and conscientiousness. Being detail oriented and a good multitasker are other important character traits. Pilots must follow detailed flight plans and go through a comprehensive checklist before taking off and a long mental checklist while flying. They monitor controls and instruments while simultaneously engaging in air combat, enemy surveillance, and/or the supervision of flight crew members, among other duties. A single mistake can cause a mission to fail and put lives at risk.

There are many variables that can go wrong during a mission. Therefore, these officers must be able to make quick, logical decisions based on the information at hand. And they must be able to stay calm under adverse conditions and intense pressure. When dropping bombs, for instance, pilots may miss their target. Rather than panic, they must be able to reassess the situation and try again. In many cases troops on the ground are counting on their success.

In addition, these men and women should have leadership skills. As commissioned and warrant officers, they serve as role models for enlisted service members. Moreover, they are responsible for the safety and protection of others, including their flight crew. It is essential that the troops they supervise trust them.

On the Job

Employers

All five branches of the military employ pilots. They can serve on active duty or in the reserves.

Working Conditions

Pilots may be stationed on aircraft carriers or US military bases throughout the world. They may take off and land on modern airfields, makeshift airstrips, and/or moving aircraft carriers. They fly in all types of weather and in combat situations. Since missions can arise anytime, they are on call 24/7. This includes weekends, nights, and holidays.

Earnings

Military pay is standardized. It is based on a service member's rank or grade and time in the service. According to the DOD, as of 2013 the base salary for active duty warrant officers ranged from $33,732 to $110,676. Annual base salary for active duty commissioned officers ranged from $34,512 to $179,700. Generally, pilots also receive an additional $125 to $400 per month flight pay, and they usually get an annual bonus that can reach up to $12,000 per year. The amount fluctuates depending on the specialty, the service member's experience, and the annual military budget. Many pilots are paid an additional $375 per month for hazardous duty. Moreover, pilots who reenlist after completing their initial enlistment may be given bonuses ranging from $25,000 to $250,000.

In addition to their salary, all service members receive benefits that can add up to a significant amount. Benefits include thirty days of paid vacation per year, free medical and dental care, education benefits, and retirement benefits. The military also provides all active-duty members who live on base with housing and food. Service members who live off base receive a food and housing allowance. The amount is based on the individual's rank, family size, and location.

Opportunities for Advancement

The military provides its members many opportunities for advancement. Each time service members go up in rank, they receive a raise in pay. Typically, this occurs every two years. Individuals can advance more rapidly based on their job performance, training, ongoing education, and promotion points, among other things. As pilots go up in rank, they can advance to flight leaders—officers who command several aircraft on a mission—then to command pilots—officers who command and lead whole squadrons and/or air facilities.

What Is the Future Outlook for Pilots?

The services employ about sixteen thousand airplane pilots and sixty-five hundred helicopter pilots. New pilots are needed annually due to changes in personnel and to replace pilots returning to civilian life. Pilots who leave the military usually find employment as commercial pilots.

Find Out More

BaseOps
website: www.baseops.net

BaseOps is an online military aviation community. It provides weather, flight, and airfield information for pilots; information about flight training, military pay, and discounts; discussion forums; and a link to a Facebook fan page.

Order of Daedalians
PO Box 249
Universal City, TX 78148
phone: (210) 945-2111
website: www.daedalians.org

The Order of Daedalians is an organization dedicated to honoring and supporting past, present, and future military pilots. It offers scholarships to high school and college students interested in becoming military pilots.

US Army Aviation
website: www.usarmyaviation.com

This website is dedicated to Army aviation. It has a photo gallery, information about aircraft, and information for aspiring pilots.

US Marine Corps: "Specialized Training: Flight School"
website: www.marines.com

This article on the Marine Corps official website gives information on Marine pilot training. Other articles on the website give information about the Marine Corps in general.

US Navy Test Pilot School
22783 Cedar Point Rd., Unit 21
Naval Air Warfare Center Aircraft Division
Patuxent River, MD 20670
phone: (301) 342-4131
e-mail: tpsinfo@navy.mil
website: www.usntps.navy.mil

The US Navy Test Pilot School trains experienced Navy pilots as test pilots. The website provides information about the training, the job, helpful links, and a photo gallery of aircraft.

Special Forces

Special Forces are the military's elite combat force. They perform clandestine, high-risk missions, which typically involve offensive raids, search-and-rescue operations, intelligence gathering, and demolitions. Special Forces members must be highly trained swimmers, divers, parachutists, combat experts, and survival specialists. Currently, since direct combat assignments are limited to men, female service members do not have the option of pursuing a career in Special Forces.

Four out of the five military branches maintain Special Forces units. Also known as Special Operations Forces or Special Ops, these fighting men include Army Green Berets, Rangers, and Delta Force; Navy SEALs; Marine Force Recon and Detachment One; and Air Force Combat Controllers, Pararescue, and Combat Weathermen. Each group has its own area of specialization. Green Berets specialize in gathering intelligence behind enemy lines. They approach their targets by sea, air, and land. Rangers parachute into enemy territory. They specialize in search-and-rescue missions. Delta Force members perform

At a Glance:
Special Forces

Minimum Educational Requirements
High school graduate

Personal Qualities
Exceptionally physically fit; willingness to face danger

Certification and Licensing
Secret security clearance

Working Conditions
All climates, weather conditions, and settings including enemy controlled areas

Salary Range
Basic pay from about $16,824 to $179,700

Number of Jobs
As of 2013 about 8,000

Future Job Outlook
Good

highly classified missions involving counterterrorism and hostage situations.

Navy SEALs also are involved in counterterrorism. They operate on sea, land, and air. They conduct rapid-strike missions aimed at capturing high-status enemy personnel throughout the world. Among one of their most famous missions was a 2011 helicopter raid on terrorist Osama bin Laden's secret compound in Pakistan, which resulted in the death of Bin Laden.

Marine Force Recon and Detachment One are often the first Americans in hostile territory. They gather intelligence about the resources of the enemy, which is used in support of all branches of the military. Air Force Combat Controllers also support other troops. They are certified air traffic controllers who set up landing strips, conduct surveillance of potential air assault zones, and guide aircraft into enemy territory. Pararescuemen are trained health care professionals and parachutists. They parachute into hostile territory to seek, rescue, and medically treat injured personnel. Combat Weathermen are trained meteorologists (weather forecasters) who support covert missions by gathering data about environmental and weather factors in enemy territory.

Depending on the service branch, in a typical day Special Ops personnel may parachute out of an aircraft into hostile territory to conduct a scouting mission. While in the field they may discharge a loaded weapon and/or participate in hand-to-hand combat. They may dive out of a small submarine in order to destroy an enemy watercraft with underwater explosives. Or they may clear a minefield. Rescuing service members trapped by enemy forces and administering emergency medical care may also be part of some of these servicemen's workday. Special Ops members also participate in strenuous practice exercises under simulated mission conditions and attend a wide range of classes in subjects as varied as Arabic language and air assault training.

How Do You Become a Special Forces Member?

Education

Enlisted personnel serving in Special Operations must have a high school diploma. Officers must have at least a bachelor's degree. To

Pararescue personnel take part in a combat insertion and extraction exercise in the African country of Djibouti. Pararescue is one of the US military's Special Forces units.

prepare for a career in this elite fighting force, in high school young men should take classes in physical education, health, and psychology. Being part of a school or intramural sports team also helps prepare aspiring troops. It provides them with physical conditioning and gives them experience in working as part of a team.

Other training takes place in the military. Special Forces applicants undergo rigorous training before being accepted as a team member. It takes up to seventy-two weeks and includes instruction in explosives handling, land and underwater demolitions, and disposal of explosive devices. Marksmanship, silent infiltration, close-quarters combat, scouting and reconnaissance methods, map reading, and survival tactics are also covered. So are mission planning, foreign cultures and languages, counterterrorism and counterintelligence, high-altitude parachuting, scuba diving, swimming, and extensive physical conditioning.

Trainees are pushed to their physical and mental limits. They are allowed little sleep or nutrition, and field training is held in extreme conditions. For example, Navy SEAL training includes an exercise held in Alaska in which trainees must jump into ice-covered water, tread water for three minutes, then pull themselves out of the frigid water without assistance. Many recruits fail to meet the challenge of training and are reassigned to the infantry or other combat specialties. In an article on the Careers in the Military website, Air Force pararescueman Lucas Ferrari explains: "The training that we do is dangerous. Rock climbing, sky diving, scuba diving are activities that some people may view as hobbies, but the military requirements and equipment involved require that pararescuemen understand the dangers of each activity."

Those service members who become Special Ops personnel must continue training throughout their military careers. They are expected to stay in top physical condition and maintain proficiency in all the skills the job requires.

Certification and Licensing

Not everyone who wants to become a team member is given the opportunity to go through training. Servicemen must prequalify for Special Forces training. In most cases this does not require a special license or certification. It does require that aspiring Special Operations members meet rigorous physical and mental requirements. For example, to qualify for Army Delta Force training, servicemen must successfully complete an all-night march over rough terrain in a set period of time while carrying a heavy rucksack. Each time the servicemen reach a predetermined goal, the distance to the next goal and the weight of the backpack are increased, while the time allotted to reach the goal is decreased. If a soldier cannot pass this early test, it is unlikely he is fit enough to complete the actual training and is therefore rejected.

Aspiring team members' mental toughness is also tested through a barrage of psychological tests that evaluate their psychological resilience and emotional stability. In addition, all prospective team members must obtain secret security clearance before being admitted to Special Forces training. Gaining secret security clearance indicates that the military certifies an individual can be trusted with sensitive information that could cause damage to the United States if it is leaked. Applicants for secret security clearance must be US citizens. They must not have a police record. And they must pass an intensive background check.

Once a service member begins training, part of training often includes instruction that leads to special licenses and/or certification.

These include certification as an air traffic controller for Air Force Combat Controllers and licensing as a paramedic for Air Force Pararescuemen. In addition, most Special Ops troops must be airborne qualified. This means they are licensed or qualified in the use of parachutes.

Volunteer Work and Internships

Young people interested in a career in Special Forces can learn about military life by participating in Junior Reserve Officer Training Corps (Jr. ROTC) in high school and/or ROTC in college. Participants receive fitness training, course credit for participating, and take part in activities such as drill and recon teams. College ROTC students also participate in summer training that may include airborne training. College ROTC members may qualify for a merit-based college scholarship in return for military service as a commissioned officer after graduation.

Skills and Personality

Special Operations personnel must be in top physical condition, and they must be mentally strong, disciplined, and determined. These men cannot crack under pressure. They should be willing and able to complete challenging missions despite obstacles, unexpected disasters, or personal injuries. To succeed they must be able to stay calm in the face of danger. This involves confronting their fears and trusting that their training and that of their team will lead to success. Even if it means risking their own survival, they must put the needs of their team and the mission above their own needs. Indeed, the job of a Special Forces member depends heavily on self-sacrifice and teamwork. A description of the personality traits of an Army Ranger on the Army Ranger Association's website explains: "Mental and physical discipline, technical and tactical expertise and a never quit mindset are some of the qualities and characteristics that set an Army Ranger apart from everyone else."

Being adaptable is also vital. No two missions are exactly the same. Special Forces operate in all types of terrain and weather conditions. They must be ready to deploy at a moment's notice. And they never know what might happen during a mission. Therefore, they should be good problem solvers who can make sound judgments and reasoned decisions rapidly when facing the unexpected.

On the Job

Employers

The Army, Navy, Marine Corps, and Air Force employ Special Forces. Team members can serve on active duty or in the reserves.

Working Conditions

Special Ops can take place anywhere in the world. Team members train and work in all terrains, climates, and settings. They may be exposed to extreme temperatures without protection from the elements. They may have to crawl through mud carrying heavy equipment on their backs, march through insect-infested jungles, dive out of small submersible vehicles, and/or parachute from aircraft at high altitudes. Moreover, missions are dangerous, and there is always a chance of injury or death.

Missions may occur at any time including nights, holidays, and weekends. These service members are always on call. Since missions are usually secret, team members cannot share with their loved ones where they are going, what the mission entails, or when they expect to return. When these servicemen are not deployed, they work and train on military bases, ships, or submarines.

Earnings

Military pay is standardized. It is based on a service member's rank or grade and time in the service. According to the DOD, as of 2013 the base salary for active-duty enlisted service members ranged from $16,824 to $89,220. For active-duty commissioned officers, annual base salary ranged from $34,512 to $179,700. Special Forces receive an additional $375 per month for hazardous duty. In addition, many receive additional compensation for special skills. For example, airborne-qualified service members are paid an extra $150 per month. Those who are scuba-diving qualified receive an additional $225 per month. Those who are fluent in certain foreign languages receive an additional $200 per month. Moreover, all service members receive benefits that can add up to a significant amount. Benefits include thirty days of paid vacation per year, free medical and dental care, education benefits, and retirement benefits. The military also provides all active-duty members who live on base with housing and food. Service members who live off base receive a food and housing allowance. The amount is based on the individual's rank, family size, and location.

In addition, upon enlisting in the military individuals who apply for Special Forces can earn a cash bonus ranging from $3,000 to $13,000. The military also offers other enlistment bonuses, which vary depending on the military branch, whether the recruit chooses active duty or the reserves, the terms of enlistment, the military career, and the enlistee's education and qualifications. For instance, enlistees with a bachelor's degree who sign on for two years active duty can earn an additional $5,000 cash bonus. Moreover, enlisted Special Forces members who reenlist after completing their tour of duty are eligible for up to a $40,000 reenlistment bonus. For officers, the bonus can reach up to $150,000.

Opportunities for Advancement

Typically, service members receive a raise in pay each time they go up in grade or rank. This normally occurs every two years. However, individuals can advance more rapidly based on their job performance, training, and ongoing training, among other things. Ongoing training also allows these men to branch off into other military career paths. And, although there are no equivalent jobs in civilian life, the discipline and leadership training that these elite servicemen receive is an asset in gaining and keeping civilian employment.

What Is the Future Outlook for Special Forces?

The military has about fifty-five hundred enlisted Special Forces team members and about twenty-five hundred Special Forces commissioned officers. New team members and officers are needed each year to replace personnel returning to civilian life. Moreover, the ongoing threat of global terrorism has increased the demand for trained Special Forces personnel.

Find Out More

BaseOps: "Pararescue: Air Force Special Operations Command"
website: www.baseops.net

BaseOps is a website dedicated to the military and to military careers involving aviation. The page on pararescue members discusses the job, training, current operations, combat gear, and the history of Air Force pararescue.

Navy SEALs
website: http://navyseals.com

The official website of the Navy SEALs provides a wealth of information about the job including information about enlisting, videos, and news.

US Air Force: "Special Ops"
website: www.airforce.com

This is the official website of the Air Force. The article on Special Ops provides information about a career in the Air Force Special Forces.

US Army Rangers
website: www.army.mil

This US Army website provides information about the Rangers. There is information about the job, Ranger school, and airborne school.

Interview with a Navy Hospital Corpsman

Neath Williams is a hospital corpsman in the US Navy. He served ten years active duty, including three combat tours in Iraq, and is currently serving in the Navy Reserve. Williams is also the co-founder of the Society of Artistic Veterans, an organization focused on connecting service members and veterans interested in the arts. He spoke and communicated via e-mail with the author about his military career.

Q: Why did you join the Navy?

A: I don't remember any moment when I decided to join the Navy. I had no foresight about what my future held. I did not see further than high school. But something in my subconscious told me that [joining the Navy] was the thing to do.

Q: Why did you become a hospital corpsman?

A: When you go in the service, they help you pick your job from your ASVAB [Armed Services Vocational Aptitude Battery exam] score. Based on my score, the recruiter suggested hospital corpsman. I was very fortunate. It was a good choice.

Q: How did you train for this career?

A: I went to hospital corpsman school in Texas. After the initial training, you get to specialize. With additional training you can go to different schools and get different certifications like respiratory therapy or radiology. I went to medical service school to learn to be a combat corpsman. There I went through Marine training, getting yelled at, crawling through the mud. You can jump around a lot with the training. You can serve with Marine Recon units or Navy SEALs. Corpsmen have a lot of opportunities.

Q: Can you describe a typical workday?

A: Every tour was a bit different. The first tour was moving forward daily as the surge of troops pushed towards Baghdad. We would get outside an area with heavy fighting and set up the Shock Trauma Platoon [a small, mobile medical unit that functions as a field emergency room for troops injured in combat] and maintain that position while receiving casualties until it was time to pack up and move forward or back. Every day was maintaining the Shock Trauma Platoon.

Second and third tour was with Navy Riverine Squadron One. I would typically get up, grab breakfast, prep my gear, attend any briefings we may have for upcoming missions and visit with my guys while they maintained their gear, guns, trucks, and boats. We did several missions a week, and some of them could take us several miles away from the FOB [forward operating base] and we could potentially stay away for days or weeks. I was responsible to my men daily and that was my number one priority. In our free time we'd read books, watch movies, and work out in the gym. I would also set up some fun events for my team, movie nights, game nights, and our little holiday parties. Nothing crazy; just some time to get our minds off war and time to relax—that's another part of being a doc!

Q: What do you like most and least about the job?

A: What I like most is my role in the unit. Everyone respects the "doc," no matter their rank. I also like being part of something, the comradery, the service to the nation, the people around you, the traditions, the uniform.

What is probably worst is that when you are in a combat situation, there's a lot of anxiety. You know all these guys. You know about their families, their wives, their children, and you care about these guys. If they get hurt you are responsible for saving their lives. The responsibility hangs heavy on me.

Q: What personal qualities do you find valuable for this type of work?
A: To do this job you need courage, perseverance, and selflessness because when you are in combat you have to think of others. You have to be someone who is willing to jump over a wall to rescue others at the risk of your own life. I don't know if it is something you know about yourself until you are in that situation. In retrospect, you go, wow, I did that!

Q: What advice do you have for students who might be interested in this career?
A: In high school, do volunteer work with firefighters. It's different than the battlefield, but having the experience helps. Even being a lifeguard or working in a nursing home. Do anything where you have to take care of other people. It will make you more valuable to the team once you become a hospital corpsman.

Q: What is one thing people may not know about this career?
A: It is very exciting and rewarding. If you are a young person with a passion for health care, if you want experiences that set you apart from your peers, join the Navy. You won't work on cadavers. You work on actual people and have actual experiences that set you apart. Every single unit in the US Navy and Marines, every ship, every diving unit, every tank unit, every Navy and Marine Special Forces unit has a Navy hospital corpsman assigned to them. There are more of us than any other rating [Naval enlisted personnel health profession]. With this career, you can do so many different things. It's like a long doorway with so many doors. There is so much opportunity. You can go forward, try new things, double back.

Other Jobs in the Military

Accounting specialist/officer
Administrative support specialist/officer
Aerospace engineer
Air crew
Air traffic controller
Armored assault vehicle crew
Avionics technician
Broadcast journalist
Chaplain
Computer systems specialist
Construction equipment operator
Dentist
Dietitian
Diver
Electrician
Fire fighter
Flight engineer
Graphic designer
Infantry
Instructor

Lawyer
Machinist
Marine engineer
Mechanic
Medical laboratory technician
Musician
Nuclear engineer
Nurse
Personnel specialist
Physician
Psychologist
Public information officer
Recruiter
Sales and stock specialist/manager
Seaman
Survival equipment specialist
Translator
Unmanned vehicle operations specialist
Weapons maintenance technician
Welder

Editor's Note: The online *Occupational Outlook Handbook* of the US Department of Labor's Bureau of Labor Statistics is an excellent source of information on jobs in hundreds of career fields including many of those listed here. The *Occupational Outlook Handbook* may be accessed online at www.bls.gov/ooh/.

Index

About the Author

Barbara Sheen is the author of more than eighty books for young people. She lives in New Mexico with her family. In her spare time she likes to swim, cook, walk, garden, and read.